JOB HUNTING. NOW WHAT?

KEEPING IT REAL IN THE MODERN CAREER SEARCH

LISA A. HOLMES, MS HR

 FriesenPress

Suite 300 - 990 Fort St
Victoria, BC, V8V 3K2
Canada

www.friesenpress.com

ISBN
978-1-5255-3878-0 (Hardcover)
978-1-5255-3879-7 (Paperback)
978-1-5255-3880-3 (eBook)

1. BUSINESS & ECONOMICS, CAREERS

Distributed to the trade by The Ingram Book Company

TABLE OF CONTENTS

To my loves, James, Brea, and Halle—
for making me believe that everything is possible.

*"When something bad happens you have three choices.
You can let it define you, let it destroy you, or you can let it
strengthen you."*

—Dr. Seuss

INTRODUCTION

MY "AHA!" MOMENT

Throughout my professional career, I prided myself on being diligent, strategic-thinking, and motivated. Each new role was methodically planned to make the right move toward my goals, and was met with enthusiasm.

In my decades of working in Human Resources (HR), I've consulted leaders about their careers and professional development at some of the best organizations. But, out of nowhere, I found myself in a job transition. How could this have happened? Not to the Human Resources lady, as I'm fondly called. I was knocked off-balance, and started to reconsider every prior move and business relationship.

Fortunately, I could rely on my human resources experience to pick myself up and launch a job search. In it, I found this maze of uncertainty and mixed messages. It's no wonder an increasing number of college students, colleagues, and friends who were in a job transition or planning the next career move were seeking my help. They were stumped, struggling, and quickly needed to make heads or tails of this crazy and unpredictable job market.

Until now, there wasn't a simple, clear roadmap of what lay ahead, where to start, and how to successfully work through the process. The goal in writing this guide is to use my decades of human resources and coaching expertise, and my own job transition journey, to educate others on the emotional and practical steps to help navigate the job search process. A wide-eye view of the process will ensure that you land your next career opportunity as painlessly as possible, as well as maintain the job in an ever-changing world.

Additionally, I have asked coaching clients to share their biggest fear and greatest learning in their process. Woven in between each chapter, their innermost thoughts have been shared. I felt it's important for you to know that others have experienced your same thoughts and feelings. Here, you will gain my coaching and insights that have helped many others to move quickly through the process, and find their next career opportunity.

CHAPTER 1

WHAT THE HELL JUST HAPPENED TO ME?

Each day, you are going along with life, working feverishly and keeping your head down. You are educated, considered a subject matter expert, and are highly respected within the organization and industry. More importantly, you love your job and the company.

Then, out of nowhere, you receive a call from Human Resources or are summoned to what seems like a strange meeting request. You're sitting in an uncomfortable, uncharted place. Soon, you are informed that the organization no longer needs your services.

The room starts to spin; you begin to hyperventilate. You see the messenger's mouth moving, but you can't understand what they're saying. The words just aren't making sense. Quietly, you are walked out the door with your years of service and your memories in a box. Downsized from the job and company that you love.

Maybe you'll be graduating from college soon. That's a huge accomplishment! The end of your college career begins a new transition to becoming a working adult. The focus is no longer on maintaining grades or managing competing projects. It's shifted to the stressful reality of entering a job search process for which you don't feel prepared.

Ladders, Inc., billed as the leading career site for jobs paying more than $100,000, cites its "Third Page" data indicating that 18.8 percent of respondents identified their boss as the main reason for job dissatisfaction. Thirty percent cited their dissatisfaction as pay-related. Even more professionals cited boredom as their pain point with their current job. Any of these factors could have eighty-seven percent of passive candidates considering whether the grass is greener on the other side of the fence, and where to navigate their career from there.

Whether you've suffered a workforce reduction, are entering the job market for the first time, or are contemplating your next career move, it's confusing and has landed you in an unfamiliar place. You might be asking yourself, "What the hell just happened to me?"

Let's face the truth and admit that this is indeed a challenging situation to be in. People who experience a substantial change or a traumatic situation are subject to five stages of grief. Even though no one has physically died in this case, the loss of your job, stability, income, and the life that you've known can feel very similar. This new reality can hit you like a ton of bricks. Many people don't experience all of these stages, or even in this order—which is perfectly normal. We all grieve differently. Some people will outwardly show their emotions. Others might express their grief internally. It is helpful to recognize these five stages of grief to be a real part of the process and use them as a guide to put context and understanding to where you are.

1. Denial and isolation

The first reaction is to deny that this really is happening. You are in utter disbelief. You can't believe that this just happened, which is a natural response to blocking the immediate shock. In this stage, we tend to tell the story of what happened over and over again. Once you start asking the question, "How did this happen?" ensure that you are moving out of this stage.

2. Anger
Brace yourself for when the reality starts to set in, and feelings of anger follow. Memories will start crashing down: *Don't they remember all of my weekends and time away from my family? I took on task that nobody else wanted to do and made them tons of money.* Or, re-enacting every detail when a hiring manager is slow to respond to your job search efforts. Be careful to control this feeling, and not take it out on yourself or others.

3. Bargaining
In this stage, we just want things back to the way they used to be. The normal reaction to feelings of helplessness causes us to rationalize things; as in, *If I had noticed the signs, I could have done something.* Or, *If I could have brought in that big deal, this wouldn't have happened.* Be careful not to stay here too long. It will keep you living in the past and unable to move forward.

4. Depression
Sadness and regret can prompt depression. We can feel that life is passing us by. Getting out of bed could be a challenge, combined with feelings of exhaustion.

5. Acceptance
Congratulations on reaching this stage, which means that you are no longer looking back. That's not to say that you will not continue to feel the vast emotions associated with your job transition. Acceptance is the beginning of the healing process and moving toward new opportunities.

Often, we tend to spend a good deal of time scripting the story of our lives; dreaming of what kind of job, salary, perks, and office we might have, and what lifestyle we want to live. Our own expectations of what life's meant to be like can paralyze us from moving forward. This guide will help you rewrite your story that looks beyond this moment, and into the next chapter of your career.

"My biggest fear is not being able to take care of myself as a single person."

—J.P. Moore

"My biggest fear is landing with the wrong organization."

—K.J. Miller

CHAPTER 2

ASSESS THE LANDSCAPE

Before moving forward, it's important to assess your career landscape. The information derived in the process will assist you in making the best career decision and avoiding wasting time moving down the wrong path. This state of awareness probably feels odd and uncomfortable. Often, we spend more time working and doing for others. This place is all about YOU. If you don't know what you want in your next role, how do you know where to find it or when it shows up?

Let's do the work. Ask yourself:

What's going on currently in my industry? Is it stable or volatile?
Does my past role fit my current needs?
What roles will I consider?
What organizations would I want to work for, and why?
Am I in the right geographic location to find my new role?
Am I open to relocation?
What work will make me feel happy, engaged, and at my best?

Benchmark Compensation
Search the internet for salary reports; the Department of Labor; payscale.com, careeronestop.com, glassdoor.com, and salary.com to

find out what others in the same role are earning. It's key to know what the top third of your targeted organizations are paying. Be sure to take your geographic location into consideration.

Oftentimes, we think more about what we used to earn. That was then, and this is now. Remember, you might have earned increases over the years, which placed you at the top of the organization's compensation scale. Gathering benchmarking information from these sources will validate whether you're on target. You must negotiate from a factual place and not based upon emotion or your living expenses. This collective information will help you as we move into the salary negotiation step that will be discussed later in the book.

Entrepreneurship

When in a job hunt, many people start to consider other options to traditional employment, such as entrepreneurship. Whether they are tired of corporate, past bad bosses, or feel that they have hit the glass ceiling, there are things to consider before jumping right in. If you are considering entrepreneurship, go into it with your eyes wide open—and for the right reasons.

What does it take to really be an entrepreneur? According to Forbes, there are "5 Personality Traits of an Entrepreneur" (Rampton, 2014). Over decades, I have been an entrepreneur of several different businesses, and I wholeheartedly agree that it takes:

1. Passion

Typically, entrepreneurs aren't in it for the money. Most work an insane number of hours for little or no pay. You are the head of everything. No one will give you direction or keep you on track and focused. So, why would they do this? Entrepreneurs are driven by solving a problem or making things easier for others

According to research conducted by Tony Tjan and co-authors Richard Harrington and Tsun-Yan Hsieh, 65% of founders have been identified as driven by "heart." Tjan also added that most entrepreneurs are fueled "by an unshakable sense of purpose."

When starting a business, there will be many highs and lows. Your passion and commitment to the mission must be able to sustain you while you're not earning a paycheck.

2. Resilience

Most first-time entrepreneurs make the assumption that their own excitement should immediately translate into business success. That's the furthest from the truth.. Even with the best plans, you might still fail. Entrepreneurs must have the ability to dust themselves off, assess the learning, and create the next strategies. If you know the stories of the world's most successful entrepreneurs—for example, Walt Disney, Steve Jobs, and Bill Gates—they experienced and overcame major trials and setbacks. To reach your goals, you must possess that same strong sense of resilience.

3. Strong Sense of Self

Entrepreneurs tell of many problems seen and unforeseen. They are aware of possible challenges with gaining funding, branding, and more. There will be setbacks along the way . Maybe a vendor relationship or selected technology isn't working out. Some way, entrepreneurs work it out.

Being self-confident and motivated are vital traits. Despite any challenges, entrepreneurs are confident and believe wholeheartedly in their ideas. According to a study by the Ewing Marion Kauffman Foundation on behalf of LegalZoom, "91% of entrepreneurs are confident that their businesses will be more profitable in the next twelve months." Many will try to discourage you from starting a business. Entrepreneurs aren't sidetracked by naysayers.

4. Flexibility

Being able to adapt to change and challenges is crucial. As new information presents itself, business plans and product ideas may change several times from when they began. Entrepreneurs should be flexible and adjust as the need arises. They aren't derailed or paralyzed but can quickly pivot to stay on course.

5. Vision

Entrepreneurs are innovators and are on the lookout to improve a service or product. They recognize issues and do something about them. In 1994, Jeff Bezos had a vision to be "the world's most consumer-centric company" in a new world of e-commerce retail. His vision is industry leader Amazon.

In 2010, my daughters, Brea and Halle, started a natural skincare business, Sweet Dream Girlz, at the ages of sixteen and ten years old. They started the business out of their frustration to find sweet, fun products for their age group. They developed a vision of who Sweet Dream Girlz was: what she liked, read, listened to, and more.

For almost six years, the brand evolved into a lifestyle for junior girls. My daughters stayed true to developing products that every girl would love. Their vibrant sneakers and apparel were sold by specialty retailers and were celebrity-endorsed.

While entrepreneurship offers freedom, greater earning potential, and flexibility, ensure that you have the tolerance and fortitude to withstand the challenging and possibly lean times.

"After 28 years, I found myself downsized. How will I maintain my home, car, living and insurance expenses for my family?"

—M. Hoskin-Redditt

"Everyone's job search is different and you can't judge yours by someone else's journey. You can't appreciate being on the mountain top unless you've been in the valley. It's okay to have a pity potty but don't forget to flush and move on."

—G. Davis

CHAPTER 3

FINE-TUNED SKILLS

Skills are one of your most important assets. Fine-tuned technical, job-related, and soft and transferable skills can give you the competitive edge needed for landing the next job opportunity.

Technical skills are the abilities and knowledge needed to perform specific tasks. They are practical and often related to mechanical, mathematical, technology, or scientific roles.

Some of the most recognized technical skills are:

- big data analytics
- programming and coding languages
- project management
- information security

Candidates with strong technical skills are viewed as people who have a good ability to multi-task in challenging and complex roles.

Job-related skills are based on work responsibilities and everyday tasks. For example, a Certified Public Accountant (CPA) will need to have auditing skills; teachers need lesson-planning skills; and electrical engineers need CAD (Computer Aided Design) skills.

Soft skills are also known as people skills. The term describes those personal attributes that indicate a high level of emotional intelligence. The list is extensive, but the most common ones that recruiters and hiring managers look for are:

- communication
- self-motivation
- leadership
- teamwork
- decisiveness
- time management
- adaptability
- collaboration
- conflict resolution
- strategic planning
- emotional intelligence
- self-awareness
- culture leader
- growth potential

As an HR professional, we applaud you for being an expert in your field. But, connecting well with others is equally as important. If you struggle in this area, it means that you have difficulty building relationships and developing partnerships, which will limit your opportunities and become a roadblock in your career.

Developing your soft skills will cause you to get out of your comfort zone and seek opportunities to stand out. One way to improve your communication would be to join Toastmasters, a national organization that offers public speaking workshops. Try demonstrating your leadership, time management, and collaboration skills by volunteering to solve an operation issue. The task could involve leading a task team across multiple areas of the business operation. Then, develop a project plan to include milestones and deadlines.

Transferable skills are those that aren't seen as belonging to any specific job or industry. These are general skills that can be transferred between jobs, industries, or departments. Employers value these skills because they can be used in many ways within the organization. When considering a new field/industry, it's important that you emphasize these transferable skills. It can go a long way to convincing hiring managers of your fit for the role, even though you might lack the job-specific knowledge.

Some transferable skills are:

- business strategy
- business acumen
- operational efficiency
- change management
- leadership
- time management
- prioritization
- delegation
- project management

Paul Petrone, editor at LinkedIn Learning, has written an article, "These Are the Skills of the Future, According to 39 Industry Experts." Petrone says, "Hence, over the next five years, with artificial intelligence and other technologies changing the market, jobs won't go away. But the skills needed to do most jobs will change (and, in many cases, change drastically)." In his research for the article, he interviewed more than thirty-nine experts across ten industries, and discovered that in the future, professionals will need these three skills:

- a growth mindset
- strategy
- employee empowerment

The article goes on to further identify the specific skills that'll become increasingly more important over the next five years in technology, marketing, sales, creative, Human Resources, management, project management, and business leadership.

Petrone's insight is helpful in working through the following exercise.

Identify your strongest four technical skills:

Identify your six soft skills:

Over the past five to seven years, what was your most used job-related skills?

In the future, what will be the industry-specific skills necessary?

It's equally as important to know your areas of challenge or opportunity. To help you gain insight, maybe speak to someone who knows you well; both personally and professionally. Their view can identify areas that might have been a blind spot for you. If needed, any of the top personality and behavior tests, Myers Briggs, DISC or Situational Judgment Tests (STJs) that employers use to gauge can be ordered online.

In order to further drive into fine-tuning your skills, think about:

What have been my professional challenges?

What technical, job-related or soft skills do I need to get better at, or learn?

When reviewing job descriptions for my desired job, what skills does it require? Do I possess them?

Should I seek a professional certification or an advanced degree? How will it benefit me professionally?

You have identified your areas of opportunity. What now? Right at your fingertips, there are numerous resources that can assist in growing your areas of professional development. Seek out workshops, webcast, YouTube videos, and classes. One of my favorite sources is Coursera, a site of more than two thousand college courses taught by top professors at the best universities.

Take this time to do the work and develop your most valuable tool—you!

"Nobody knows everything but, I am capable. As long as I stay open, I will just keep learning."

—K. Price

"Change can be difficult. But, if you want what you want, it's necessary! In the midst, remain positive."

—C. West

CHAPTER 4

DEVELOP A SMART SEARCH STRATEGY

Each day of your job hunt must be approached with purpose, and successfully set up to yield fruit. A wise person once said, "What gets planned gets done." Maybe you are someone who actively analyzes, set goals, and moves on to getting things done. Or, perhaps you haven't given it thought because it takes too much time and effort.

It's the truth. Developing a SMART strategy will take time. Once you have done it a few times, you will soon agree that it's vital—not just in your transition, but in your daily business. The SMART strategy begins with the end goal in mind. Consider where you are today, the gap between here to the end goal, and what's needed to accomplish it.

As an HR practitioner, I am often amazed to discover that business leaders have been unsuccessful at a job or at accomplishing important goals, as a result of failing to have a SMART strategy.

How does developing a SMART strategy help you?

- provides a clear focus on your goals and intentions
- effectively uses your time only on things that need to get done

- writing things down will give you peace of mind
- provides clarity to knowing that you are getting closer to your goals
- helps to measure how effectively you are moving toward your goals
- provides ease in communicating your goals to others, their contribution, and needed support

Let's break this down further. SMART is defined as:

S	SPECIFIC	Specify a task to be completed
M	MEASURABLE	Is this task measurable and how will it be evaluated. This will help indicate when the task has been accomplished.
A	ACHIEVABLE	Is the task achievable and what are the resources and actions required to achieve this task?
R	RELEVANT	Is the task relevant to achieving the particular stated priority in the eLearning plan and relevant to the school's current circumstances?
T	TIME BOUND	How long will the task take and in what timeframe will it be achieved?

In part, the table of contents and areas of opportunity discovered in the Assessing the Landscape chapter serve as a great start to the SMART strategy. I challenge you to dig deep. Take this time to hone the skill of planning. Going forward, use it to create the vision and priorities in your new role and business. Cascading this process down to your direct reports is highly advised, to ensure that you will meet your goals.

Later, it can act as a tool for validating your own job performance. End each day with reviewing the SMART strategy and identify goals for the next day. The ability to proactively plan will ensure that you stay on track to finding your new job and increasing your value through professional development.

ACTION PLAN

GOAL 1	ACTION STEP DESCRIPTIONS	PARTY / DEPT RESPONSIBLE	DATE TO BEGIN	DATE DUE
Write your goal statement here.				
List Resources & Desired Outcomes.				

GOAL 2	ACTION STEP DESCRIPTIONS	PARTY / DEPT RESPONSIBLE	DATE TO BEGIN	DATE DUE
Write your goal statement here.				
List Resources & Desired Outcomes.				

GOAL 3	ACTION STEP DESCRIPTIONS	PARTY / DEPT RESPONSIBLE	DATE TO BEGIN	DATE DUE
Write your goal statement here.				
List Resources & Desired Outcomes.				

GOAL 4	ACTION STEP DESCRIPTIONS	PARTY / DEPT RESPONSIBLE	DATE TO BEGIN	DATE DUE
Write your goal statement here.				
List Resources & Desired Outcomes.				

CHAPTER 5

MENTAL AGILITY

Going through a job hunt can be taxing. The countless hours spent combing the internet, applying to postings, and making phone calls can take its toll. The impromptu interviews and multiple résumé revisions are downright overwhelming. And, the unacknowledged résumés and phone calls can be disheartening.

The mental agility required in a job search can be easily compared to that of an athlete. Have you ever wondered how someone could bike one hundred miles in high altitudes, mountain board on all types of terrain, or surf waves up to fifty feet high? These athletes have relentless mental agility.

Athletes can withstand pain, dig deep within themselves to find strength, have a strong sense of competitiveness, and refuse to quit. There will be days when the phone won't ring. Or, you're sitting on the edge of your seat awaiting a call about a possible opportunity or interview. These silent times can be nerve-wracking. Negative self-talk won't benefit your career. It's crucial that you keep positive thoughts and avoid the habits that lead to negativity and unhealthy behaviors. Choose to have conversations with positive-minded people who can help by being supportive.

Developing your mental toughness and endurance will keep you working your SMART strategy and preparing to land your dream job. Now, you ask, "How do I develop mental agility?" Start practicing these good habits.

Emotional stability

Sometimes, our emotions are hard to control. Realize that it is only temporary and give yourself a moment to process them. Then, assess how to react to them. To get on the right track, ask yourself:

What are the positives about the situation?

Is my current viewpoint objective?

Perspective

Perspective is everything. See the lesson in every situation, and you will grow internally and emotionally. Learn how to keep things in perspective and not overreact.

Readiness for change

Many have said that change is the only constant. Therefore, flexibility and adaptability are the keys to success. If one strategy doesn't work, don't keeping doing it and expect a different outcome. Change your course of action.

Detachment

Remember, it's not about you and taking things personally. Don't worry about "Why me?" Focus on what you can control.

Develop the right attitude toward setbacks

Complications and setbacks are a part of life. Minimize the damage, accept the lesson, embrace the process, learn from it, and release yourself from the issue.

Breathe

When stressed, try not to immediately react. Stop, take a step back, and breathe through the issue. As you breathe, your troubles will seem less intense.

Focus

Maintain your focus on the short- and long-term goals. Put them in places where you will see them daily. If you are inspired, create a vision board of your goals or SMART strategy.

Patience

Don't expect to see immediate results, or rush things. A job search is a process that can take weeks or months.

Control

Your emotions don't have to be the master of your life. If you become aware of your thoughts and emotional triggers, you can intentionally control your thoughts.

Acceptance

Don't bother with things that you can't control. Your time is better spent controlling your mindset, attitude, and responses.

Never give up

Remember the athlete mentality? You can't move forward if you give up or stand still. Keep it moving.

Take care of you

Love and take care of yourself daily. Develop a regular de-stress routine. Simple things like taking a walk, practicing yoga, and movie-watching can combat stress. There are several free apps that teach meditation and calmness. If you find yourself stressing, pop in your earbuds and gain a moment to just be still and yield to the process.

At some point in life, we all had hobbies. Whether it was sports, crafts, or music, it gave us a creative outlet; offered new challenges and promoted physical health. It's never too late to reconnect with a past hobby or create a new one.

Practicing a faith has exceptional benefits too. I agree with the experts who say that it creates an increased sense of well-being, hope, and optimism.

A strong sense of direction

Difficult times aren't a good enough reason to lower your standards. Set your bar high, and work to achieve and maintain it. Don't be desperate and accept whatever comes.

If there are times when you might feel off-base or less centered, you have the ability to redirect yourself. Quickly, get back to these steps.

"Now, I realized that my employer only saw me as a body and someone replaceable. I learned that my value was relative. Ultimately, I can never get comfortable in a job ever again. I need to be primed and ready to look for better opportunities. And, be loyal to myself first."

—M. Hoskin-Redditt

"My biggest fear is of the unknown. I'm very organized and I like to plan. Not knowing what my employment situation will be makes it difficult to plan too far in advance and causes anxiety."

—A. Donato

CHAPTER 6

CREATING AN HR-BELOVED RESUME

Nobody can underestimate the importance of having a stellar résumé. First impressions count. A lasting impression that you make with an employer depends upon your résumé presentation. A stellar résumé must clearly tell your career story.

Recruiters will spend only seconds reviewing your résumé. Therefore, it's imperative to present yourself well. In this competitive job market, your résumé must contain the right information, keywords, and highlighted achievements that will ensure you stand out among the countless others.

Regardless of what you've read or heard, avoid playful fonts, lingo, and over-complicated formatting. Sticking with a 12-point Arial font will get the job done.

Applicant Tracking Systems or ATS

Before diving into creating the résumé, it's important to first understand the Applicant Tracking System, or ATS. The ATS is the central location and database where employers will post job openings, and manage résumés and applicant information. Initially, your résumé isn't read by a recruiter or hiring manager.

First, the ATS aligns or parses the keywords in the job that you are applying to, along with those in your résumé. Revisit the job posting to look at the job requirements, including the training, skills, and abilities they are seeking. Include words they use without going overboard. Only use them where it makes sense.

Then, the system ranks or qualifies your résumé according to the number of keywords in it; thus placing you in a favorable position to be reviewed further by the recruiter or hiring manager. According to LinkedIn, fewer than thirty percent of people applying online receive a response, and fifty percent of applications are screened out by the ATS.

Selecting a Résumé Type

Depending upon your circumstance, the most commonly used résumé types are:

- Chronological
- Functional
- Combination

A *Chronological* résumé is widely used, showing your employment history in a timeline. This type works best if you have had a stable work progression and can show how you've received increased responsibility with each role. Most employers prefer this style.

A *Functional* résumé has become almost obsolete. HR hates it because they need to draw their own conclusion, which isn't ideal. The functional résumé format was created to cover up gaps in an applicant's experience. Since it has been used less and less, most find it odd. Odd could shoot you in the foot.

A *Combination* or *Hybrid* résumé has space at the top of the page for skills and accomplishments. Unlike the functional résumé, it leaves the bottom half for a more traditional approach to the work history, where each position is accompanied by a blurb that outlines responsibilities and accomplishments.

Which type of résumé is best depends on the situation. Choose the format that best represents you in the context.

For years, candidates have been instructed to keep a résumé to one page. I suggest that a résumé should be as long as it needs to be to show that you're the best fit for the position. Employers will spend limited time reviewing your résumé—which is why you need to be concise. Write concise accomplishment statements. Eliminate fluff and jargon. Only say what is necessary to sell yourself. As a rule of thumb, if you have less than ten years of work experience, your resume should fit one to two pages. If you have more experience (or the job requires more unique skills), a two- to three-page resume could be a better portrayal of your experience.

Resume Must Dos

1. Contact information: Your name, address, phone, email, and LinkedIn link should be accurate and in larger font than the resume body.

2. Summary statement: In a few sentences, summarize your experience, professional qualifications, and value added to an organization. The summary is often to referred as the executive summary. For advanced roles, this is critical information to show your success in a similar role.

3. Core proficiencies: This is a list of skills and behaviors that are specific and well-defined, and used to lay out an employee's performance expectations (i.e. strong writing skills, expert analytical skills).

How to quantify performance

It's not enough to tell the interviewer that you did this or that in your role. It matters more about the success measures you demonstrated. To quantify your performance, think of it this way:

- Did you make money for the company?
- Did you increase market share?
- Did you improve your ranking in comparison to other departments, branches, or competitors?
- Did you suggest any ways to cut costs in your team, department, unit, branch, or company?
- Did you regularly meet all your deadlines? Within what time frame?
- Did you improve the efficiency of your job, team, or department?
- How did your performance compare to prior years?
- How did you rank against the competition?
- How did you rank against industry averages?
- What were your performance goals? Did you meet them? Exceed them? How did you contribute to the bottom line?

The guide below is another great source to measure your skill proficiency. When considering each of your competencies or skills, at what level were these tasks executed?

Proficiency Level	Proficiency Level Definition
Level 5-Expert	Applies the competency in exceptionally difficult situations. Serves as a key resource and advises others
Level 4-Advanced	Applies the competency in considerably difficult situations. Generally requires little or no guidance
Level 3-Intermediate	Applies the competency in difficult situations . Requires occasional guidance
Level 2-Basic	Applies the competency in somewhat difficult situations. Requires frequent guidance
Level 1-Awareness	Applies the competency in the simplest situations .Requires close and extensive guidance

The majority of your résumé-writing time should be spent on writing compelling accomplishment statements. There are helpful verbs to use when writing your accomplishment statements. Always start your accomplishments with a verb.

Here are a few to consider:

Designed	Developed	Launched	Spearheaded
Reduced	Yielded	Accelerated	Amplified
Boosted	Delivered	Lifted	Merged
Modified	Grew	Replaced	Supervised
Trained	Projected	Assessed	Promoted
Oversaw	Improved	Adapted	Directed
Managed	Solved	Initiated	Controlled
Coordinated	Executed	Produced	Built

Summary Statement

A summary statement or résumé profile contains a few statements that highlight your qualifications for the job. It serves as a precursor to the rest of your résumé, and encourages the hiring manager to want to learn more about you.

Remember to include:

- Relevant core strengths and skills
- Past experiences with key functions of significance
- Notable accomplishments that can be replicated in this role

Job-Hopping

Over the past decade, we have seen a shift in the economy, which has resulted in job-hopping being on the rise. Often, recruiters and HR professionals have frowned on candidates who have had multiple jobs within the past five years.

In some cases, job-hopping is out of your control and even necessary. The goal is to get ahead of any misunderstanding or perceptions about the job changes. If this is your scenario, adding a career transition overview directly after your résumé might be warranted.

A career transition overview provides one to two lines explaining the reason behind each job change. For example:

CAREER TRANSITION OVERVIEW
Alton Financial Corp
Chief Talent Officer
The organization had fallen upon financial challenges, which resulted in outsourcing the HR function.

Micro Tech, Inc.
Global HR Executive
The organization sold its technology, which didn't result in a long-term opportunity for me.

Stella Cosmetics, Inc.

Sr. HR Director

Accepted role with Micro Tech, Inc. to broaden my skill set to lead global HR teams in the U.S., Latin America, and the U.K.

If you decide not to do it on your own, hiring a professionally-qualified résumé writer might be an option. Before moving forward, ask these questions:

1. What are the résumé writer's academic credentials?
2. How long have they been a résumé writer?
3. Does the résumé writer belong to The National Résumé Writers' Association?
4. What have they done to position themselves as an expert in the industry, and share their writing?
5. Can they provide client testimonials?
6. Will they provide you with a sample of their work for your review?

For additional information, I suggest that you review the following sites:

- The National Résumé Writers' Association
- Professional Association of Résumé Writers and Career Coaches

The purpose of the resume is to get you an interview. Most people think that will land them a job. I am here to tell that it won't. Employers will want to check you out through a series of interviews and assessments.

Chronological Resume Example

Calvin Miller

17017 Hampden Ct, Edmond, OR 00222

c: 455-999-3333 | e: jch1@copxs.net

https://www.linkedin.com/in/jamescalvin/

PROFESSIONAL SUMMARY

An energetic and motivating leader with a proven ability to effectively manage both staff and long- and short-term projects. A self-starter and strong independent professional who excels at analyzing products and procedures in order to generate new ideas that improve efficiency and production quality. A reputation for being highly adaptable to ever-changing circumstances and to shine when working in team environments. Advanced skill in developing and executing strategic business plans for both small and large businesses.

PROFESSIONAL EXPERIENCE

Comfort, Inc.,

Operations Manager   20XX-Present

Comfort, Inc., a $1-million foam insulation company servicing diverse industries with locations in seven states.

Manage daily operations. Train and supervise work crews in more efficient product installation techniques, resulting in reduced material waste by 20% and labor hours by 43%.

Instrumental in developing sales team's knowledge in the areas of building science and energy conservation, in order to provide customers with the information to successfully plan for and utilize spray foam insulation.

Developed an effective marketing campaign and restructured product pricing/discounts resulting in an 80% bid acceptance rate.

Implemented new bidding process utilizing Excel spreadsheets to formulate 20% more accurate bids. Allowed for the tracking of individual job costs and provided feedback on the efficiency of crews regarding material waste and labor hours.

United States Marines

Manager   (20XX–20XX)

Data Network Manager

Managed command and control data network used to generate video representation of geographic area surrounding the ship. The team consisted of thirty-eight individuals from four departments.

Production Control Officer   (19XX–20XX)

Coordinated the efforts of 135 personnel utilizing thirty-seven thousand man-hours. Completed 520 jobs totaling over $4-million during a thirteen-month refurbishment period.

Assistant Command Duty Officer   (19XX–19XX)

Directed daily routine utilizing a duty section of six hundred personnel from twelve different departments.

Instructor Pilot   (19XX–19XX)

Administered, coordinated, and supervised flight and academic training for the United States flight training program that encompassed more than two hundred instructors and six hundred students in five units.

Coordinated and supervised four Flight Commanders to ensure that pilot completion rates met quarterly and annual goals.

Managed and scheduled eleven instructor pilots and thirty-eight flight students to complete primary- and intermediate-level flight training.

EDUCATION AND TRAINING
M.B.A. in Finance, Auburn University

B.A. in Business Economics, University of Costa Rica

Aviator – Advanced Flight Training, United States Flight Patrol

Integrated Project Team Course – Project Management College, United States Flight Patrol

Selective courses in building construction, construction management, and cost estimating.

AWARDS AND COMMENDATIONS
Navy Marine Corps Commendation Medal (two)

Navy Marine Corps Achievement Medal

Combination Resume

JENNIFER RIVERS

1543 Central Park Drive ~ New York, New York 10001

212.555.1212   pro@news.net

MARKETING EXECUTIVE

Product Launches ~ Overseas Partnerships ~ Presentations

Accomplished, multilingual Professional consistently recognized for achievement and performance in the fuel industry. Innovative and successful in mining new sales territories and establishing business alliances, including the recent partnership with *MJM Oil* in Korea. Proven leader with special capabilities in building teams, strategizing, and implementing workable marketing plans employing television, radio, Internet, and print media. Fluent in English, Korean, Japanese, and French.

BUSINESS SKILLS

Marketing

- Launch gasoline exports in conjunction with new production plant start-up; target overseas markets.
- Initiate sales of ULS, an environmentally-friendly new product launched in the European market.
- Establish joint venture partnerships in Europe and Far East; implement marketing for aviation fuel and asphalt as a value-added commodity.

Market Planning

- Analyze regional import / export economics and the interregional oil markets.
- Participate in contract negotiations for strategic alliances with major European and Asian concerns.
- Achieved $25 million in revenue by developing offshore storage programs that fulfilled seasonal market trends in the region.

Product Planning

- Optimize production mode by selecting appropriate refinery; research product specification revisions by country.
- Propose and participate in the Plant Operation Committee, a team effort between production and sales.

PROFESSIONAL EXPERIENCE

TTR CORPORATION, New York, New York   1993 – Present
Vice President, Overseas Business Division
- Promoted to position in March 1996; selected as one of three employees to attend an MBA course in 2003.
- Named *Employee of the Year* in 1996 based on professional achievements.

FUEL INDUSTRY OF AMERICA, New York, New York   1989 – 1992
Manager of Marketing
- Provided analysis on fuel industry, drafting report for the White House.
- Awarded the *Honor Prize* in 1992 based on performance evaluations of oil producers.

EDUCATION

UNIVERSITY OF NEW YORK, New York, New York
Bachelor of Arts in Communications, 1988

To Cover Letter or Not Is the Question

Cover letters have had their day, but are now considered mostly dead and behind the times. Why the change? Recruiters have resolved that they all read the same. Therefore, they never bother to spend the time reading them. The traditional cover letter has evolved and been replaced with an e-note; a less traditional communication sent in the body of an email.

In the world of quick communication, you must write your job search communication in a short, concise format. At this point of the interaction, the potential employer doesn't know you and is struggling with whether to move you forward to a phone interview.

You should instantly connect with the reader. Don't overwhelm them with a long, lengthy message filled with unimportant details. An e-note has become most popular.

Written in the body of an email, your e-note should follow this structure:

- In the subject line, indicate the title of the role for which you are applying, or something key about yourself: e.g., Jane Doe, A, CMA, CFP
- Get quickly to the point and create grammatically correct, engaging content. Stick to two or three strong paragraphs
- Use three to five bullet points to highlight expert experience and achievements
- End the note with your contact information, LinkedIn profile, and online portfolio

Not to speak out of both sounds of my mouth, but there is still a place for the cover letter. When applying to job postings that allow for an uploaded cover letter, take the time to provide a clear overview of why you are a fit for the role.

Sample e-note

Subject: HR Generalist Applying for HR Manager Opportunity

Mr. Green,

Your HR Manager position intrigued me because of the dual focus on HR generalist function for the entire organization in tandem with staffing, training, and organizational development for new ventures. That combination closely aligns with my experience for the past five years with Micro.

SNAPSHOT:
HR Generalist; SHRM-SCP; Eight Years in HR with Five Years in Management
BS and MBA Degrees in HR

HR MANAGEMENT PROFILE:
Recruitment, Staffing, Training & Development, Employee Relations, Benefits & Compensation, HRIS, Organizational Development, Regulatory Compliance & Reporting, Budget Administration

I'm available to interview via phone, Skype, or in-person, so let me know what works best for you. Once you've reviewed my attached résumé, you'll see that I'm well qualified to take the reins of your HR organization and meet your aggressive growth and performance improvement goals.

Thank you,
Annie Lexington, SHRM-SCP
555-555-5555
annielex@gmail.com
linkedin.com/in/annielexHR.com

CHAPTER 7

DON'T HIDE, GET CONNECTED

While in the job hunt, you will need to be connected to the world more than ever before. The ability to cast out a wide net to your family, friends, colleagues, vendors, and professional organizations will provide endless networking opportunities in your job search.

For some, telling people that you're looking for a job can be awkward. Be mindful of your approach. Here are a few tips to help convince people to be your ally in the job-hunting process.

Be Strategic In Your Communication

I know that it would be easier to send out one mass email to all of your contacts about your job search. Don't do it! Everyone won't be able to assist you. And, save yourself the daunting task of having to respond to two hundred emails from folks who will repeatedly ask the same questions or share their job hunt experience. You aren't looking for someone to commiserate with.

You will need to be intentional about whom you engage, and know how each person can help you. Consider emailing: "Hi Pam, I am looking to use my twenty years of experience as a project manager, ideally within the consumer products industry. I know that you have worked with some of these organizations and wondered if you would be open to sharing my resume with them?"

Attend Networking Events

These events are perfect for growing your network and reaching into your target organizations. The Balance published an article that included some compelling statements that highlight the value of networking:

- 70% of people in 2016 were hired at a company where they had a connection
- 80% of professionals consider professional networking to be important to career success
- 35% of surveyed professionals say that a casual conversation on LinkedIn Messaging has led to a new opportunity
- 61% of professionals agree that regular online interaction with their professional network can lead to the way to possible job opportunities

Source the event calendar of professional associations or use the online social networking service, Meetup.com, and Eventbrite to join in-person group meetings. Even if you aren't a current member of the professional association, ask to attend a one-time meeting as a guest.

At the event, avoid running around the room and handing out your business card. Ask a regularly attending member in the room whom should you be introduced to. Seek out one or two meaningful connections. The member might offer to go and make the introduction for you.

When meeting someone for the first time, ask thoughtful questions about their work, latest projects, and interests to get the conversation going. If you're someone that struggles with small talk, a few suggestions are:

- What brings you here?
- What do you do for a living?

- How are you enjoying the event?
- How did you hear about the event?
- I'm always nervous to attend these if I don't know anyone. How about you?

Subtly, ask to keep in contact and possibly exchange your contact information. As not to get confused with whom you met, jot down some small takeaways from the conversation to prompt your remembrance.

If it's someone that you want to engage further, follow up with an email shortly thereafter to say:

> "Hi Kenneth, it was nice getting to know you at the Certified Public Accountant networking event. I remembered that you told me about how much fun you had on your latest fishing trip. I noticed in the paper this upcoming fishing show and wanted to share it with you."

The next time you reach out, Kenneth would be receptive to a coffee meeting or speaking about your career interest. Building new relationships takes time. Don't devalue its importance.

Develop Your Branding Pitch

These days, everything and everyone is a brand. It's no wonder that the elevator pitch has evolved into what is called the branding statement.

A branding pitch is your thirty-second to convey who you are, what you do, and what you're looking for. In Chapter 2, "Assessing the Landscape," you have already identified the role that you will be targeting. Next, write down a few key skills or accomplishments that you would want others to know about you. When people are listening to your pitch, they are thinking, *What's in it for me to know you?* Your goal is to make them want to hear more.

Here is an example:

> "I am a human resources professional with a strong passion and talent for identifying high-potential people and developing them into successful leadership roles. My success has led me to work for world-class organizations. I have admired XX Company and its reputation, and would like to speak further about leveraging my passion in a senior talent development role with your organization. Would you be open to arranging a <u>quick</u> call with me next week?"

Your branding pitch has to position you as an expert. It should feel natural and not like annoying sales call.

Use Social Media
Social media sites can help you find unofficial job openings. They have become the way for professionals to network and meet hundreds of people. Start by maintaining a comprehensive and up-to-date profile. Ensure that your email and profile photo are a professional representation of your brand. Follow your targeted organizations and join professional groups. Often, they actively post job openings for its members.

I encourage you to tweak your branding pitch slightly and post it inside LinkedIn groups to say:

> "I am a human resources professional with a strong passion for identifying high-potential talent and developing them into successful leadership roles. My success has led me to work for world-class organizations. I am looking for my next opportunity to leverage my skills in a senior talent development role. Please contact me at: (email address)"

This will open a discussion among the group members. Be engaging and respond in a timely way to everyone who contacts you.

Creating your own content and sharing interesting articles and observations are ways to attract more followers. Daily, I receive connection requests because I share my thoughts on a subject via social media. The more followers you have can get you closely connected to influencers and decision-makers.

If you aren't social media-savvy, search for videos and webinars on using social media tools to increase your knowledge and skill. Make time daily to increase your social presence.

Connect Inside the Organization

As a single job is posted, it's not uncommon for hundreds or even thousands of candidates to apply. For example, recruiters could elect to only review the résumés of the first twenty or so applicants. As you can see, your probability of getting seen can be low.

I suggest that you get savvy. After some research, compile a list of your targeted employers. Then, use the professional network, LinkedIn, to identity the recruiter, positions hiring manager, or leader. Even connect with someone at the organization that would be your peer, boss, and an executive leader over your potential business unit.

Send a connection request and make sure to use the "Add Note" feature to share why you are looking to connect with them specifically. This will likely help you to start a conversation with them.

In your message, ensure that you state briefly how your experience relates to the targeted role. Lastly, request a quick phone call to discuss your career success and the role. The message could read:

> "Hello, Emma. This is Phillip Williams. I know that you are busy, so I will be brief. I was excited to learn of the VP, Public Relations role with your organization. I have more than ten years of successful PR experience working for a competitor, XYZ Co., and would like to share more with you about my successes. I wondered if you would be

available on Tuesday for a quick call around 2:00 p.m. Please confirm at your earliest by reaching me at xxx-xxx-xxxx, or email at phillip.williams@gmail.com."

You will be amazed that some will immediately respond and accept your invitation.

It's helpful to identify organizations that will align with your latest discovery. Search the internet for the national and local "Best Places to Work" list, business journals, and recently recognized companies to identify places that you will target based upon your wish list. The "On the Move" announcements in newspapers and journals are an excellent way to discover unpublished roles that may have been vacated due to someone moving up or out of a position.

"To WIN at life you have to HUDDLE up with the RIGHT people."

—Pastor Reginald Steele

"Despite being in HR and telling others to always be networking, I never made it a priority for myself. Since being in my personal job search, I have been forced to network and surprised to find that I actually enjoy it."

—A. Donato

industry nice industry influential lies nice
untrue negative lies EVASIVE NARROW MINDED nice
rude lies advisor persuasive rude advisor
negative face to face
lies lies FACE TO FACE lies rude lies nice
dishonest CONTRACT RUDE phone interview
advisor NICE advocate LIES lies
rude RECRUITER RUDE nice
lies nice influential
informative contract rude lies pushy NICE
manipulative interview nice
rude RUDE industry NICE untrue untrue
nice lies
disrespectful independent lies PARTNER
lies resourceful nonresponsive dishonest nice
interview nice trustworthy influential lies
nice EVASIVE
trustworthy interview resourceful nice
Recruiter slow moving partner
rude empathetic untimely nice
nice nice EMPATHETIC lies

CHAPTER 8

NOT ALL RECRUITERS ARE CREATED EQUAL

In your job hunt, it's likely that you will be contacted by recruiters who will be offering jobs with all kinds of organizations. What I'm about to say might sound strange coming from someone in HR. But I, too, have personally experienced some bad recruiters. From colleagues, I have heard interesting stories about their recruiter encounters of the bad kind. In all fairness, there are some good recruiters out there too. They are a necessary part of the process if you best understand:

- Types of recruiters
- What to expect
- How to identify a good recruiter

Type of recruiters
Internal recruiters are employed with or are contractors of the company. They aren't commissioned, are less aggressive, and are expected to represent the company well. Not only are they focused on aligning a candidate's experience to the role, they are seeking how you will fit with their organization.

A contingency recruiter is an outsourced provider used by companies to locate, screen, and interview candidates on their behalf. Job seekers don't pay them a fee. They are paid by the client organization and seldom are decision-makers to determine if you get the job or not. They are most commonly called headhunters.

As a result of a workforce reduction, displaced employees can be assigned an outplacement recruiter. An employer offers this benefit to help workers find resources in their job search. These firms provide resume-writing, job interviewing tips, and career counseling services. Rarely will they have access to job opportunities.

What to expect
Recruiters are task-driven and not paid to be your friend. They aren't career counselors and won't lend insight about where you fit into an organization.

The recruiter's job is to:

- Post job openings
- Source candidates
- Interview
- Make the job offer

A good recruiter
There are some awesome recruiters out there, too. At the outset, they are clear about the job description, client organization, challenges within the role, compensation structure, and company culture. A good recruiter will have a substantive conversation with you to best understand your background, skill set, and interest. Once the recruiter has secured an interview for you with the company, they will offer insight into the organization and help you prepare for the meeting.

They're great at keeping you informed, and walk step-by-step with you during the process. The recruiter provides you with timely information and feedback. Basically, you know that they know. They go the extra mile to keep you engaged and interested in the role. And, they act as your advocate.

Be mindful that you are in control of whom represents your personal brand. Every recruiter relationship might not be a fit for you. Keep your eyes open and trust your gut.

"I graduated college in 2007, which was the largest economic downfall since the '70s. One of my greatest fears was having gone through school and being left behind. Competition is fierce and if you aren't in it, then you're a step behind the pack. You're constantly playing catch-up with the rest of your peers."

"In addition, I experienced being fresh out of school and unemployed several times while in my twenties. A large stressor was learning to deal with student loan lenders and bill collectors. They don't teach you about that in school. That's all real-world experience."

—J. Dean

CHAPTER 9

THE SECRET WEAPON

In preparing for the interview, consider developing a career portfolio. This tried-and-true method is your way of presenting your progress, achievements, and contributions in the best way to prospective employers. Leave the portfolio behind with the prospective employer for them to take a look at, even after you have left the interview. I guarantee that few candidates make this kind of a presentation.

What is a career portfolio?

- A visual representation of your skills, abilities, and qualities
- A tangible collection of your progress, achievements, contributions, and efforts
- Provides "evidence" of your potential by demonstrating what you have accomplished

What should be in the career portfolio?

Whatever you choose to include is up to you. More is not better. Consider things only of significance. In a simple, clear front, three-prong folder, include:

- Résumé

- Professional philosophy/mission statement: A short description of the guiding principles that drive you and give you purpose
- List of accomplishments: A detailed list that highlights the major accomplishments in your career to date
- Samples of your work: A sampling of your best work, including reports, white papers, studies, brochures, projects, presentations, etc.
- Letters of recommendations: A collection of any kudos you have received from customers, clients, colleagues, past employers, professors, etc. Include copies of favorable employer evaluations and reviews
- Awards and honors: A collection of any relevant certificates of awards, honors and scholarships
- Professional development activities: A list of professional associations and conferences attended and any other professional development activities
- Military records, awards, and badges: A list of your military service, if applicable
- Volunteering/community service: A description of any community service and/or volunteer work you have completed, especially as it relates to your career

Recruiters and hiring managers will love that you've done the work for them. You've provided them with insights about your capabilities and what others say about you. Being memorable means that you'll have a better chance of getting the job.

Relatability Factor

Contributed by Janis P. Moore, PHR, SHRM-SCP

You have probably heard the saying, "People buy from people they like."

This is a very true statement. When purchasing a product or service, most people would never buy from a person that they thought was rude or disrespectful. Nor would they buy from someone that they really couldn't relate to. Well, the same things happen in the job-hunting process. A person that the hiring manager can't relate to, or see in the role, or as part of the team, will never get hired—regardless of their skill set, degrees, pedigree, university affiliation, or anything.

Every day, talented candidates apply for roles that they are qualified for on paper. They have an incredible amount of talent. Unfortunately, talent alone will not get you hired, neither will skill. In most cases, there is only one winner. Many of those not selected, wonder:

- Why were they hired over me?
- What skills did they have?
- Was it their degree?
- Was it their pedigree?
- Do they have a relative or friend that gave them the nod?
- Who do they know?
- Did they get a degree from Harvard, just like the hiring manager or CEO?
- Is it because of their ethnicity, race, or creed?

While all of those things may have been considered, the final decision can often boil down to the likeability factor. For the purposes of this section, likeability is synonymous with relatability.

In Molly Reynolds' article, "Want to Close the Deal? Make Yourself More Relatable," she discusses how we can use the words "likeable" and "relatable" interchangeably. She says, "in order to move your audience (hiring manager) to action, you must be able to relate to them." This means that in every interaction with a hiring manager or member of the hiring team, you must be able to identify with them on a personal level. Failure to relate to them will result in a negative experience by you and/or the hiring team, which will result in the "thank you for your time" email.

Some of Reynolds' other tips to help us become more relatable include: communicating with authenticity, keeping calm, and relying on relationships. She says that when you uncover common interests, you will both naturally show enthusiasm, and build bonds and trust that are bigger than your professional relationship. It is truly important that you are relatable, and therefore, likeable in order to close more deals—or in this case, to get hired—and build lasting relationships in your profession.

Sadly, many high-potential candidates aren't hired because they aren't able to relate. As a candidate, you have to be relatable to everyone you meet—from the receptionist to the most senior person you interact with. Each one of them might have to give the sign of approval for you. This relatability is particularly difficult for women and people of color.

Likeability is different from being professional or cordial. This is also related to how you show up for the interview. In the old days, a candidate would never show up to an interview without wearing a skirt or pants suit in navy, black, or gray. Today, depending upon the company's culture, a candidate can wear almost anything to an interview that's not jeans or tennis shoes or flip-flops, and be hired.

Showing up in a suit and tie for a man or showing up in a skirt or pants suit may also cost you the job. As a candidate, you may be too formal in a not-so-formal environment.

From a distance, it is very difficult to know the exact environment you are going into—and therefore, you need to do your research.

Doing research may be something as simple as going online to see if you can find videos of the organization you are attempting to work for, that show the environment and its workforce. If that doesn't work, you can go the business or send a friend to watch the employees going in and out of the business. This simple step of understanding the environment can prove to be invaluable.

For example, in the south and the northeast U.S., a man would not dare to show up for an interview not dressed in a business suit, white shirt, and a tie. In California, a man who shows up in a business suit, white shirt, and tie will very likely not be hired. As a candidate, you need to be a person who can fit into the environment. Fitting in may also be comparable to the statement, "When in Rome, do as the Romans do." This also means, when in Rome, dress as the Romans do. Being overdressed is just as bad as being underdressed.

If, for some reason, you can't go to the interview location in advance to perform your reconnaissance work, it is imperative that you dress in layers that can be removed. For example, a jacket that can be taken off, pantyhose that can be removed, a tie that can be taken off, etc. All of these are just as key as what you say during the interview.

To be more relatable, we suggest that you also avoid:

- bragging or too much self-promotion
- name-dropping
- gossiping
- being emotionless or using stoic facial expressions
- sharing too much information too soon

In a study conducted at UCLA, subjects rated over five hundred adjectives based on their perceived significance to likeability. The top identified adjectives were sincerity, transparency, and capacity for understanding another person. According to TalentSmart, a provider of emotional intelligence (EQ) test, training and research data to more than 75% of Fortune 500 companies, it was discovered that people who possess these fourteen skills are likeable and highly outperform those who lack the skills.

Let's test your emotional intelligence in this area:

1. Prove that you are listening by asking thoughtful questions
2. Fully commit to the conversation by putting away your phone
3. To gain trust, be genuine
4. Eliminate preconceived notion. Be open-minded
5. Don't attention-seek. When recognized, appreciate those that helped you get there
6. Be emotionally and professionally consistent and level
7. Use positive body language and enthusiastic tone of voice
8. Leave a strong first impression by having a strong posture and firm handshake
9. Use their name throughout the conversation
10. If you want people to like you, smile naturally
11. Open up without sharing too much personal information and confessions
12. Touching lightly on the shoulder shows that you care. Be careful that it's welcomed
13. Balance passion and fun to capitalize on valuable social moments
14. Network with ease and promote harmony in the workplace

CHAPTER 10

THE INTERVIEW

Interviewing for a job is never easy, no matter how solid your qualifications or references. Lead with a positive mindset. Your preparation and performance during the job interview will make or break you landing that dream role.

Know the company
It's well advised to know the organization with which you are interviewing. One way a company shows how it stands out is through its mission or values. Take time to view its site and understand the mission, company size, locations, history, and what's important to it. It can be a commitment to delivering superb client services, or sustainability. In the interview, you can speak about this and how your personal experience or values align with those of the organization.

While on the site, take a peek at the investor relations information. For publicly-held companies, you should be able to access the annual report. The valued information will disclose new product ventures, company risks and whether revenues are growing or stable.

Often, younger, growing organizations will communicate their corporate news through blogs or video messages. Whether it's a post to announce a new addition to the team or the latest product development, you should know about it.

Aside from knowing as much as possible about the company, it's a good idea to be able to speak about the industry as a whole, and it's impressive to speak about the competition and how the company fits into the bigger picture.

View the organization's LinkedIn company page and scroll down to the "Other Companies People Viewed" section to identify the organization's competitors.

All your research will not be in vain. Your goal is to express your enthusiasm for the company, and why you should work there.

Prepare your story

During the interview, it's likely that you will be asked behavioral interview questions. They most often start the phrase "Tell me about a time when. . ." Interviewers are looking for you to respond with specific examples as they relate to past experiences, rather than with generic answers. At the root of this interview style is the belief that your success in the past is a predictor of future behavior.

As you are formulating your response, be sure to include this three-component process:

1. The task/situation

    This is the background and context in which you acted. What was the problem that you needed to solve? How did you recognize there was a problem?

2. Action

    The action is what you did or said in response to the situation and how you did it. Commonly, these are the steps that you took to resolve the task/situation. Who did you partner with to resolve the matter? What resources did you use?

3. Results

After you identified the task/situation and developed an action plan, what was its outcome? How did you know that you were successful?

The most common behavioral questions are related to:

- leadership
- teamwork
- handling conflict
- problem solving
- biggest failure
- work ethic
- biggest accomplishment

It's important to keep in mind that there are no right or wrong answers. Often, the interviewee will respond with their prepared script. Yet, they miss the mark by failing to hit the points that the interviewer is seeking in the response. Remember to listen carefully to the interviewer. Directly answer the question and be clear and detailed in your response. Framing your responses in a conversational way comes off more genuine and confident. This makes your interview more memorable. Stay away from generic responses. These are the ones that an interviewee found by searching the best interview questions online, and they lack substance. It's your time in the light. Make it count. If you use the three-component process, you can't go wrong.

Identify three business task or situations using the three-component process.

New interview tools and techniques

The traditional interview has been the standard for decades. As HR professionals, we realize that it doesn't demonstrate the candidate's full capabilities, weaknesses, or eliminate interviewer bias. The latest interview tools to come on the scene are:

- soft skills assessments
- job auditions
- meetings in casual settings
- video interviews
- virtual reality assessments

Likely, you might be asked to take an online assessment. Online assessments will measure a candidate's soft skills that were covered earlier in the book. An employer might invite you to work a day or accept a temporary contract to observe your skills in action. Casual interviews over coffee or dinner will lend insight to your character and conduct outside the work environment. Recorded video interviews will reduce the number of in-person interviewing. These videos can be easily shared with hiring managers. Virtual reality assessments is the latest trend. Candidates are placed in 3D environments to test their skills.

What not to say

In my years of interviewing candidates, I am amazed how they sabotage themselves simply by what they say and share. Be conservative and keep your focus on your skills and qualifications as they relate to the job.

The interviewer wants to know why you are the best-qualified person for the job. Here is a short list of things not to say, and why not to say them:

1. Refrain from using slang or profanity. Keep it professional and polite.
2. Don't speak negatively of your former employer or job. An interviewer might think, *Will you say that about the new one?*

3. Don't speak negatively of your past boss or coworkers. The interviewer could assume that you're unprofessional.

4. Don't share too much personal information. It's dangerous and can be a turnoff. One could wonder if you can you be trusted with confidential information.

5. Never verbalize that you're nervous. It will appear that you lack confidence.

6. Never minimize your work experience. Let the interviewer determine that. Focus on the skills that you do have.

7. Avoid using clichés and buzzwords. They won't offer insight into who you are, or your knowledge.

8. Avoid using filler words, such as "like" and "um." It could be perceived that you lack the communication skills to engage well with clients.

9. Don't share your political views. It can make the interviewer uncomfortable.

10. Don't use acronyms. It can isolate the interviewer if they are unfamiliar with them.

11. Don't ask to see the benefits package or vacation. Wait until you are offered the job.

12. Never ask how long the interview will last. It appears that you really don't want the job, or that you poorly planned your schedule.

13. Never ask about an alternate work schedule. Again, wait for the job offer before having this conversation.

14. "It's on my resume." It might be. But the interviewer wants to hear it from you.

15. "No, I don't have any questions." They hear that you've had enough. Or, they think that you arrived unprepared for the interview.

Preparing thoughtful questions

Before the interview ends, you will be asked if you have any questions for the interviewer. Preparing thoughtful questions demonstrates that you have taken interest in the organization and are serious about working there. Also, it's your opportunity to interview the hiring manager and see if it's the right organization for you.

Here are a few questions to pose:

- "What things have others in the past done to succeed in the role?"
  Understanding what the expectations will be and how the organization measures achievements, is insightful.

- "How has this position evolved?"
  This will let you know whether this job is a dead end or a stepping stone.

- "How would you describe the company's culture?"
  This is a broad view of the organization's corporate philosophy and whether it prioritizes employee happiness.

- "What have you enjoyed most about working here?"
  Your future boss will share what's important to them. It will be interesting to see if you share the same values and see yourself working for them.

- "Over the next ninety days, what will be my top priorities?"
  This will help you make the right impression on your new job.

- "If I accepted the role, what are some challenges that I would face?"
  You owe it to yourself to know what's ahead of you. If the interviewer is transparent, you will know if the department is short-staffed, whether people work long hours, etc.

- "When thinking about others who have progressed well in the organization, what was the common quality that they possessed?"
  This question shows the interviewer that you want a long-term future with the company.

- "Why is the role available?"
  It is best to know if the vacancy was due to someone being unhappy in the role, or if they were promoted.

- "Do you have any hesitations about my qualifications?"
  This will let the interviewer know that you are open to discuss anything or clear up any misunderstanding that causes them concern about moving forward with hiring you.

- "Can you tell me what steps need to be completed before your company can grant an offer?"
  This is an opportunity to understand the timeline for a hire.

- "How is the company living up to its core values? What's the one thing that the organization is working on to improve itself?"
  This will shed light on the organization's shortcomings. And, it demonstrates your interest to understand the internal workings of the company.

That dreaded question

I can guarantee that you will be asked the question, "Why are you looking for a job now?" You might be asked several variations of the same question, such as, "Why did you leave your most recent position?" Your reason will always be important to an employer. Answering the question can seem awkward so, be prepared. Even practice your response in advance. Otherwise, you might come off dishonest or risky, even if you have nothing to hide. They're inquiring to find out:

- Did you leave for a good reason?
  They want to know if you left for something of substance or
  on a whim. Are you a loyal person?

- Did you leave voluntarily?
  They're listening to see if you were let go for performance or
  integrity issues.

- Did you leave on good terms?
  Whatever the reason, show that you left on amicable terms
  and that you value maintaining good relationships.

If you are currently employed and looking to leave your organization,
you could stick to the general rule and say that you are leaving for
a better opportunity or are seeking greater challenges. Follow up
the statement by expressing the positive reasons for considering this
new role.

Here's another sample answer:

> "I really enjoyed my time working with XYZ Marketing and
> am proud of the campaigns that I conceived and managed.
> However, I think it's time for a change. For a while, I have
> been considering working for a larger organization that
> would offer me more growth opportunities. This role seems
> like just the right fit for my background and the challenge
> that I'm looking for."

In some situations, you will have to share more information; such
as, the company sustained a workforce reduction. Even so, you
can emphasize the positive by stating that you had a respectable
tenure at your prior organization, while weaving in a few of your
accomplishments. End by saying, "When one door closes, another
of greater opportunity opens." And, "I'm looking forward to my
next challenge."

Here's another sample answer:

"Unfortunately, the company's biggest client went out of business, which had a major effect on revenues. As a result, some roles were eliminated. I'm proud of the work that I accomplished, and my former boss is one of my strongest references."

Things happen, and maybe you were involuntarily terminated or fired. If it was for performance reasons, mention any extenuating circumstances and avoid placing blame on others. Maybe the job expectations changed after you were hired, or new management took over. Make that clear.

Here is a sample answer:

"After getting a new department manager, it became clear that her expectations didn't match with my strengths. Ultimately, she decided to bring in someone who had more experience. It taught me that my talents lie in process management, and I know that I would add value in a role like this one."

At that point, highlight a few successes that you have had in process management. You have remained neutral and concise in your response. Then, redirect the conversation to something positive.

Whatever the reason that you were separated; you should make it a point to highlight the lesson learned. The goal is to put the interviewer at ease that you aren't a risk; rather, you're an experienced professional with a lot to offer them and a new role.

Let's practice right now.

Why are you seeking a new job opportunity now? Write out your response here.

Follow up

With more than several decades in Human Resources, I have seen many things change. But, the one that remains necessary is an old-fashioned Thank You note, sent via email or handwritten note. Standard practice is sending it either the same day, or the next. Forward a Thank You to all of your interviewers. This is one last opportunity to sell your qualities and skills and fit for the role. Also, invite them to your LinkedIn page to see your recommendation or online portfolio.

Ghosting

You might have heard the term "ghosting" as it relates to dating. Now, it's becoming a big problem in the interview process.

Maybe you have exchanged a few emails, performed a task, and had several interviews. Then, suddenly, the lines of communication go cold. For these reasons, you never hear from them again:

1. They have identified another internal or external candidate that they feel is a better fit.
2. They have placed you as a backup in case the #1 candidate falls through.
3. The hiring manager places the position on hold.
4. They are uncomfortable with telling you honestly where you stand.
5. They are avoiding the dreaded question, "Can you give me some feedback?" for fear of being sued.

The Ultimate Hiring Statistics surveyed 20,000 professionals around the world and found that 94% of candidates want to receive interview feedback. Yet, only 41% of respondents have received feedback before. Either way, it's disrespectful of someone's time and effort, and a poor representation of the organization. Yet, it happens.

Undoubtedly, rejection hurts. Do send a follow-up email kindly asking for an update. Don't stalk the person. This won't help you land the job. If you have been searching for some time, it can be hard not to take it personally. Consider it a gift to have had this experience before accepting the job. If the job were meant for you, it would be yours. Refocus, and spend your time preparing for the right job and organization.

"Taking into consideration my education, experience, work ethic and abilities into a new work ethic. My biggest learning has been to value myself as opposed to letting them place value on me."

—B. Maxwell

"I have embraced the power of having time to make decisions that work for my greater good and not just an immediate financial comfort."

—F. Miller

CHAPTER 11

THE SALARY NEGOTIATION DANCE

The salary negotiation process can feel like a tango. Both of you will come to the dance with the right moves. You will need to come to the interview with your best choreographed dance steps to ensure that you win.

According to Payscale's salary survey, 57% of its respondents have never negotiated for a higher salary. And, 28% of candidates fail to negotiate because they are uncomfortable or lack negotiation skills, and 19% don't want to come off as being too pushy. Or, maybe you're unemployed and feel a little desperate to get back to work. These steps will get you comfortable with the process.

Use the data
In Chapter 2, Assess the Landscape, it was advised that you benchmark your targeted roles with glassdoor.com, Robert Half, etc. These sources will disclose salary range based on position and geographic location.

When entering the interview process, this data serves as leverage. It comes from a realistic and credible source to back up your value proposition.

Early in the conversation, recruiters will ask about your salary expectations or current compensation. While they will be curious about it, you aren't obliged to share. Now, or in the near future, there are eight states that have banned employers from asking about a candidate's salary:

- California (effective January 2018)
- Delaware (effective 2017)
- Massachusetts (effective July 2018)
- New Orleans banned inquiries about all city departments and employees who work for the city
- New York (effective 2017)
- Oregon (effective January 2019)
- Pittsburgh banned city agencies from asking about candidates pay history (effective immediately)
- Puerto Rico (effective March 2018)

Remember, the first to give away a number is placed at a negotiating disadvantage.

Here are a few ways to respond to the salary history question.

Options to respond

Recruiter: "What's your current salary?"
You: "I'm being considered for, or would consider, positions that are in the range of $_K to $_K."

Recruiter: "My client will want to know exactly what you are earning."
You: "I understand the need for this information. I would be interested in hearing more about your client's budget

for the role. My salary history is confidential. But, if my range of $_K to $_K is acceptable to your client, I would like to continue our conversation. Or, at this point, I'd rather learn more about the organization and how to best leverage my talents to bring value. Should we come to an agreement that the role is a fit, then we can further discuss salary expectations."

Recruiter: "What's the lowest salary that you are willing to accept?"
You: "I am considering offers in the range of $_K to $_K."
Recruiter: "Let's make a deal. Tell me your lowest number."
You: I understand that you are working in the best interest of your client. But, undervaluing my skills and abilities isn't how I would want to start a relationship with a new employer."

If the recruiter insists or you feel uncomfortable, don't be afraid to walk away. This is a red flag and signals that the organization tries to save money by not paying its workforce fairly.

How to negotiate for more

Everyone wants and need to earn more money. I have been there too. Oftentimes, we just don't know how to ask. Here is the secret sauce. Based upon your benchmarking data, select the highest salary and make that your lowest negotiating target. If the employer has decided that you are their selected candidate, they are likely to grant it. Only use this tactic after receiving the formal offer letter. Expect some pushback, but don't take it personally. Be prepared to sell your qualities that make you distinctive and valued.

Here is what to say after receiving the formal offer:

"Thank you for the opportunity to work for XYZ Company. I am excited to leverage my talents and add value to the team. I appreciate the offer of $_K but, was expecting $_K based upon (here is where you sell your qualities, experience, drive and performance). Can we agree to a salary of $_K?"

Boost your compensation more

For many reasons, employers might not be willing to negotiate salary. There are ways to boost your compensation without increasing your salary. Be creative, yet reasonable. Here are few ideas of what to ask for:

- increased relocation expense
- increased vacation time
- flexible work hours
- ability to work from home a few days
- one-time sign-on bonus
- support of continued education/certification
- professional association membership
- gym/wellness programs

Often, these perks are on the table for discussion. Yet, very few candidates know to ask for them. In fact, a 2016 survey from the human resources association WorldatWork found that 76% of organizations surveyed have sign-on bonuses. It's a matter of getting comfortable with the ASK.

Sometimes you will win some and sometimes you'll lose some. That's okay. Be wise and look at the total picture of what you stand to gain. You win by gaining a great new opportunity with a solid organization and all its offered benefits. In the process, never come across as entitled, disrespectful or adversarial. After one or two negotiation dances, the employer will be ready to move on to establishing your start date. Or, to rescind the offer if things go too far. It's important that everyone feels good about the decision.

YOU'RE READY.

NOW, BE GREAT!

Congratulations! You have covered a ton of valuable information in this guide. I believe that if you use these steps and self-reflective questions, you will find, and be best prepared for, your next career opportunity. As you move forward, here are some ways to maintain your new job in an ever-changing economy.

Calculated risk

Calculated risk is healthy. Take advantage of opportunities that will best position you in your career and organization. Don't charge into everything that presents itself. Take a step back and assess the risk and reward involved. To weigh your options, make a list of potential risks and courses of action aligned to the risks. This approach will ensure that you aren't preceding based on emotion or held back by fear. And, ask yourself, does the reward amplify my personal brand?

Deliver results

Nowadays, employers are looking at profit per employee. If they don't see profit, they will soon consider making a change to someone new. Therefore, it will be important to position yourself as someone who delivers quantifiable results. If you or your team fails to deliver as expected, be agile enough to quickly pivot your course of action to successfully achieve your goals.

Continue to use the SMART planning tool in your business. It will provide clear direction along with your successes.

Be a problem solver

Top performers aren't afraid to not only point out problems; they are willing to jump in with both feet to find a solution to fix them. Do the research to fully understand the scope of the problem, the financial impact, and the future reward if your plan was adopted. Be a proactive problem solver.

Own your professional development

Long gone are the days of coming to work and having guaranteed employment. Business and positions evolve. Therefore, top performers should actively develop new skills. They take on new situations, wade into uncharted waters, and willingly place themselves in uncomfortable positions. They recognize that investing time in learning new things makes them more valuable to the organization, more helpful to their teammates, and more marketable in future situations. Stay curious and remain open to new opportunities.

Adapt to the technology revolution

There is no doubt that technology is changing the workplace at a rapid pace. A superabundance of online courses and workshops can provide the path. For example, General Assembly of offers a variety of courses and training options in web development, data science and digital marketing in cities around the world. With a shortage of technical talent, employers are willing to invest in growing their own. Those professionals who possess or have the willingness to gain the right technological skills will be in high demand.

Think from an abundance mindset

It's likely that much of your work will involve participating as a member of team. If you want to contribute your best effort, help your team members win, and avoid isolating yourself from your colleagues, work on your mindset and your behaviors will follow. Recognize that the pie can be big enough for all to win, and your winning doesn't require someone else on your team to lose.

Find a mentor or professional coach

Having a professional mentor or professional coach is priceless. This is someone who's experienced and knows the ropes. If done right, the relationship will yield many benefits.

A mentor or professional coach:

- challenges you and gives you insights to take better control of your career
- educates you on how to accept feedback, enhance communication and leadership capabilities
- better understands the organization's culture and unspoken rules, which can be critical to your career success
- can provide access to their own contacts and sphere of influence
- can validate your credentials and reputation
- gives steady doses of tough love—whether you want it or not

Develop a strong personal brand

In your organization, a strong personal brand has a great return on investment. You will take the branding message and skills assessments created earlier in the book and amplify them. Ask yourself what you want people to think of when they hear your name. Is there a certain subject matter in which you want to be perceived as an expert, or are there general qualities you want linked to your personal brand?

Continue to seek opportunities that will enhance your brand and be able to quantify your uniqueness. Tactfully share your success with others.

Stay ready

Keep your resume and social presence updated with new positions and accomplishments. There is an easy approach to this. Once you land a position, cut and paste a modified version of the job description into your résumé. As you have successes, add them as bullet points. In the event you need it, you're ready. By now, you have mastered the art of networking. Don't isolate yourself from the world outside of your organization. Let the newly-found connections organically grow, which will strengthen your reputation inside and outside of the organization.

In this process, you should have been reacquainted with yourself, and even awakened in many ways. I challenge you to maximize your new momentum. Continue to seek out opportunities that will leverage all your talents and skills to reach your full potential. You are the CEO of your own career.

Now, go be great!

LEADERS WITH A SCARCITY MINDSET	LEADERS WITH AN ABUNDANT MINDSET
Resource constrained	Prioritize better
I win/you lose	I win/you win = we all suceed
Lack of trust	Trust = relationships
I have the answers	Together, we can find the answers
Cost control	Investment with a return
Focus on costs	Focus on results
Buy time/hours	Buy desired outcome/results
I expect bad news	I expect high performance
Micromanagement	Stewardship
Stress and frustration	Confidence and success

"Change is inevitable. Growth is optional."

—John C. Maxwell

NOTES

Chapter 1: What the Hell Just Happened to Me?
1. *Ladders Third Page.* "Beyond the Résumé: Motivations for Making the Big Career Move."
2. "The Ultimate List of Hiring Statistics." LinkedIn. 2014. https://business.linkedin.com/content/dam/business/talent-solutions/global/en_us/c/pdfs/Ultimate-List-of-Hiring-Stats-v02.04.pdf
3. Julie Axelrod. "The 5 Stages of Grief and Loss." https://psychcentral.com/lib/the-5-stages-of-loss-and-grief/

Chapter 2: Assess the Landscape
1. John Rampton. "5 Personality Traits of an Entrepreneur." *Forbes.* April 14, 2014. https://www.forbes.com/sites/johnrampton/2014/04/14/5-personality-traits-of-an-entrepreneur/#3f67b49c3bf4

Chapter 3: Fine-Tuned Skills
1. Paul Petrone. "These Are the Skills of the Future, According to 39 Industry Experts." *LinkedIn The Learning Blog.* September 25, 2017. https://learning.linkedin.com/blog/future-skills/these-are-the-skills-of-the-future--according-to-39-industry-exp?trk=lilblog_01-02-18_PULSE-Skills-Companies-Need-Most_tl&cid=70132000001AyziAAC

Chapter 6: Creating an HR-Beloved Resume
1. Alison Doyle. "How to Write a Resume Summary Statement With Examples." June 29, 2018. https://www.thebalance.com/how-to-write-a-resume-summary-statement-2061034

2. "Action Verbs for Your Resume." https://resumizer.com/action_verbs.htm

To Cover Letter or Not Is the Question
3. Tiffany Hardy. "Formal Cover Letter or E-note? Staying Flexible Amidst Changing Expectations." October 1, 2015. https://www.bluesteps.com/blog/cover-letter-vs-enote
4. Wendy Enelow. "Cover Letter Trends: Introducing the E-Note." August 8, 2017. https://www.shrm.org/resourcesandtools/hr-topics/talent-acquisition/pages/2017-cover-letter-trends--introducing-the-e-note.aspx

Chapter 7: Don't Hide, Get Connected
1. Alison Doyle. "The Importance of Career Networking." August 23, 2018. https://www.thebalancecareers.com/top-career-networking-tips-2062604

Chapter 9: Relatability Factor
1. Molly St. Louis. *Inc.* October 2, 2014. https://www.inc.com/molly-reynolds/want-to-close-the-deal-be-relatable.html
2. Travis Bradberry. *Forbes.* January 27, 2015. https://www.forbes.com/sites/travisbradberry/2015/01/27/13 habits-of-exceptionally-likeable-people/#419104f91b1
3. Treehouse Partners. "The Likeability Factor." February 26, 2015 http://thetreehousepartners.com/likeability-factor/

Chapter 10: The Interview
1. "The Ultimate List of Hiring Statistics." LinkedIn. 2014. https://business.linkedin.com/content/dam/business/talent-solutions/global/en_us/c/pdfs/Ultimate-List-of-Hiring-Stats-v02.04.pdf

Chapter 11: The Salary Negotiation Dance

1. Jen Hubley Luckwaldt. 2016. http://www.payscale.com/
   salary-negotiation-guide/whats-holding-you-back-people-
   who-ask-for-raises-earn-more
2. "Bonus Programs and Practices." A Report by WorldatWork.
   July 2016. https://www.worldatwork.org/docs/research-
   and-surveys/survey-brief-survey-on-bonus-programs-and-
   practices-2016.pdf

Chapter 12: You're Ready. Now Be Great!

1. Rebecca Koenig. *U.S. News.* April 2, 2018. https://money.
   usnews.com/money/careers/applying-for-a-job/arti-
   cles/2018-04-02/how-workers-can-adapt-to-the-technology-
   revolution

CPSIA information can be obtained
at www.ICGtesting.com
Printed in the USA
LVHW090830310821
696489LV00003BA/309